TEACHER
INTERVIEW QUESTIONS & ANSWERS

BY ANTONY STAGG & DIANE LLOYD

THE **TESTING** SERIES
expert advice on interview preparation

how2become

Orders: Please contact How2become Ltd,
Suite 2, 50 Churchill Square Business Centre, Kings Hill, Kent ME19 4YU.

Telephone: (44) 0845 643 1299 - Lines are open Monday to Friday 9am until 5pm.
Fax: (44) 01732 525965.
You can also order via the email address info@how2become.co.uk.

First published 2011

ISBN: 978-1-907558-70-2

Copyright © 2011 Antony Stagg, www.brightsparkstraining.com

bright
sparks

Typeset for How2become Ltd by Molly Hill, Canada.

Printed in Great Britain for How2become Ltd by
Bell & Bain Ltd, 303 Burnfield Road, Thornliebank, Glasgow G46 7UQ.

CONTENTS

WELCOME

Dear Sir/Madam,

Welcome to Teacher Interview Questions and Answers: your new definitive guide on how to pass the interview process that is relevant for teaching posts within the UK. This guide has been designed to help you prepare for and pass any type of teaching interview.

Interviews can be a very nerve-wracking experience. The way to overcome those nerves is to embark on a period of intensive preparation in the build up to your interview. The majority of schools and educational establishments will assess you predominantly against the job description or the person specification for the teaching job that you are applying for. Whilst reading this guide we strongly advise that you have a copy of these important documents at your side.

If you would like any further assistance with your preparation for any kind of job interview, assessment centre or selection process, then we offer a wide range or products and training courses at the website:

www.how2become.co.uk.

Finally, you won't achieve much in life without hard work, determination and perseverance. Work hard, stay focused and be what you want!

Good luck and best wishes,

Antony Stagg & Diane Lloyd

THE **TESTING** SERIES

CHAPTER 1
INTRODUCTION

Before we get into the main element of the guide and in particular the interview questions and answers, it is important that we explore the interview process and how you can greatly increase your chances of success in applying for a teaching post.

Most educational employers are seeking teachers who are enthusiastic, knowledgeable, confident, reliable, well organised, self-motivated, hard-working, committed and loyal. By understanding what an interview panel are looking for in a successful candidate you will be increasing your chances of success dramatically. Before you go into any interview, you should always try to put yourself in the shoes of the interviewer. What are they looking for in a teacher, what are the key qualities required to perform the role competently, and what does the job description say? Once you have the answers to these questions then you can start to prepare effectively for the interview.

IMPORTANT QUALITIES AND ATTRIBUTES YOU SHOULD CONSIDER

The following words and phrases will undoubtedly be relevant to the role of a teacher and you should try to demonstrate these qualities and attributes during the teacher interview:

- Organised
- Adaptable
- Flexible
- Ambitious
- Enthusiastic
- Self sufficient
- Trustworthy
- Reliability
- Ability to teach
- Ability to adapt your teaching style to suit the class, student or school
- Passionate
- Disciplined
- Caring
- Conscientious
- Able to communicate effectively
- Knowledgeable

The above list is certainly not exhaustive; however, it will give you a great starting point in your preparation.

WHAT IS A TEACHING INTERVIEW?

A classroom teacher will almost always be asked to teach a 20 – 40 minute lesson at interview. This particularly applies if you are a (NQT) Newly Qualified Teacher or relatively in-experienced in the teaching profession. For more senior roles such as Deputy Head Teacher or Head Teacher it is less likely you will be required to perform a lesson.

Prior to the actual interview you will be given a tour of the school or college, in some cases this will be done by senior members of staff often with older students who will also have questions prepared and give feedback as part of the interview process.

PREPARATION FOR THIS LESSON IS KEY.

> If you don't think you have enough information on the lesson or interview itself – always ask the school for more.

> Never presume that resources such as paper or photo-copying facilities will be available to you.

> Always have hand-outs and resources ready and make sure you give a copy to staff that are observing your lesson as well as the students, this includes a copy of your lesson plan.

> Always have a back-up plan, just in case anything goes wrong with technology that you plan on using.

During the lesson

> Look for an opportunity to demonstrate your classroom management skills – however small and no matter how well behaved a class is – you must be able to demonstrate this at some point during your lesson.

> Establish a relationship with students – learn their names.

> Display your subject knowledge

> You must set extension work for the students – not homework but an opportunity for further learning, this could be through website or article research.

TOP TIP: Demonstrate your subject knowledge and use of praise. Show that by praising students you can achieve positive reactions and improved performance.

An interview is a tool used by the employer to assess a candidate's potential to perform a role. Unless you are an internal applicant who is seeking a promotion or sideways move, the interview will normally be the first time that the employer has the opportunity to meet you. They will want to assess whether or not you have the qualities required to perform the teaching role competently, experience in a similar role, and also whether you will fit in with a team and whether you are likely to fit into the educational team environment.

Many interviews now will be structured around the fact that the interviewer will only assess you against your responses to the questions that are asked of you. It is vital you obtain a copy of the person specification and job description for the teaching role you are applying for. This will enable you to not only be fully prepared for the interview, but it will also enable you to predict some of the interview questions! More on this later.

The interview is your opportunity to shine and with there being more and more applicants for every post available, it is vital that you try to cover every eventuality. The interview is your chance to show the employer that you are the person for the job and that you will do all that you can to perform above and beyond expectations, if successful.

Just by being at the interview you should naturally be enthusiastic about the prospect of working for the school, college or university. Why be there if your heart is not in it? The psychological element of an interview is very important. Preparing mentally for the interview is just as important as researching the educational establishment. Being in the right mindset will help you to perform at your best. There are many things that you can do to ensure you are in the right frame of mind, both immediately prior to the interview, and in the weeks and days leading up to it. Some of these include walking, running, swimming or general exercise, eating healthily and also avoiding alcohol or junk food. To the majority of people, these small changes won't seem worth the effort. However these small changes can make a massive difference to your mindset and self-confidence.

Matching the job description and/or the person specification

Before you start preparing for the interview you must get a copy of the job description and person specification for the teaching job you are applying for. The vast majority of employers will assess you primarily against these important documents. Your first task is to try to think of areas where you match the job description and person specification. You will see on the following page that I have provided you with a sample job description for a teacher. Following the job description you will notice that I have provided you with a number of 'key evidence areas'. These areas are the ones that I suggest a candidate who is being interviewed for this post focuses on during his or her preparation. It is vital that you can provide evidence of where you match the job description for the role that you are applying for.

TEACHER JOB DESCRIPTION

- Implement activities that contribute to a climate where students are actively engaged in meaningful learning experiences.

- Identifies, selects, and modifies resources to meet the needs of the students with varying backgrounds, learning styles, and special needs.

- Assists in assessing changing curricular needs and offers plans for improvement.

- Maintains effective and efficient record keeping procedures.

- Provides a positive environment in which students are encouraged to be actively engaged in the learning process.

- Communicates effectively, both orally and in writing, with students, parents, and other professionals on a regular basis.

- Collaborates with peers to enhance the teaching environment.

- Models professional and ethical standards when dealing with students, parents, peers, and the community.

- Ensures that student growth and achievement is continuous and appropriate for age group, subject area, and/or programme classification.

- Establishes and maintains cooperative working relationships with students, parents, and schools, as measured by the school survey results.

- Assumes responsibility for meeting his/her course and school-wide student performance goals.

- Ensures student progression.

- Participates in training and presentations about online teaching.

- Meets professional obligations through efficient work habits such as: meeting deadlines, meeting schedules and coordinating.

- Performs other duties and responsibilities as assigned by their supervisor.

All work responsibilities are subject to having performance goals and/or targets established as part of the annual performance planning process or as the result of organisational planning.

Once you have read through the above sample job description, take the time to read the following key evidence areas.

KEY EVIDENCE AREAS

1. Provide examples of where you have implemented instructional activities that contribute to a climate where students are actively engaged in meaningful learning experiences. An example of the type of interview question you could get asked is as follows:

Q. Can you provide an example of where you have taken it upon yourself to improve the learning environment for your students?

2. Give examples of where you have modified instructional resources to meet the needs of the students you are teaching. An example of the type of interview question you could get asked is as follows:

Q. Can you provide an example of where you have altered and changed your teaching style or lesson plan in order to adapt to a students needs?

3. Provide evidence of where you have assisted in assessing changing curricular needs and offered plans for improvement. An example of the type of interview question you could get asked is as follows:

Q. Can you provide an example of assessed or analysed your teaching curriculum and offered ideas or suggestions for improvement to the senior teaching staff or head teacher?

4. Provide details and evidence of your record/admin keeping procedures. A sample question would be as follows:

Q. Can you provide us with details of how you organise your working day and how you manage to stay on top of your admin work, marking and student records?

5. Provide evidence of how you have previously created a positive environment for your students. An example of a type of interview question would be as follows:

Q. Please provide evidence of a specific scenario where you actively encouraged your students to participate in the learning process?

6. Provide details and evidence of how you communicate with students and different groups both in writing and orally. A sample question might be:

Q. Please provide details of how you communicate effectively with your students, their parents and also other members of staff?

7. Provide evidence and examples of how you have maintained professional standards. A sample question might be:

Q. Can you provide an example of where you have challenged professional standards that you thought were lacking?

8. Provide examples of where you have supported and implemented continuous development amongst your students. An example interview question is as follows:

Q. Can you provide details of how you have previously supported professional development amongst a student?

9. Provide evidence of successful goal-setting that is relevant to your curriculum. A sample question might be:

Q. Can you provide details of how you go about setting goals for yourself and your students that are in-line with the curriculum?

10. Have an understanding of and an input in, online teaching. An example question might be:

Q. How have you been actively supporting online teaching?

11. Provide details and evidence of how you successfully manage your workload. A sample question might be:

Q. Please provide specific details and evidence of how you manage large workloads whilst working under pressure?

TOP TIP: Obtain a copy of the job description and person specification for the job you are applying for. Then, work through each element and predict the possible interview questions you could get asked. Many of the interview questions will come from these important documents.

Let's now take a look at some important aspects of pre-interview preparation.

PERSONAL APPEARANCE

This carries far more weight than people think. First impressions are so important. It says a lot about who you are. Remember that you only get one opportunity to create a first impression. Unless it is specifically not required you should always dress in proper formal attire such as a suit and tie or equivalent if you are female.

Your shoes must be clean too, and if you need a haircut, then get it done a few days before. You should prepare the night before the interview and lay everything out pressed and ready for the morning. Even down to your underwear, which sounds ridiculous, but it is all about limiting the stress that you will already be under on the day of your interview. The last thing you want to be doing is rushing around for your clothes or shoes on the big day only to find you threw away those smart shoes months ago!

You should also take a look at the website of the educational establishment you are being interviewed for. What are their brand colours? You may wish to wear a tie or some other element of your clothing that symbolises the colours of the educational establishment. This is a subtle way of demonstrating your commitment to their brand and identity.

TRAVELLING TO THE INTERVIEW

Before travelling to the interview, ask yourself the following questions:

- How are you going to get to the interview?
- Do you know where you are going to park?
- Are the trains or buses running on time?
- Do you need a congestion charge ticket if in London?

These are all obvious questions but important nonetheless.

Again, it is all down to preparation. Remember to take a contact number with you just in case you are going to be late for the interview. Then you can call them well in advance to tell them you will be late due to a breakdown or traffic congestion. If you are travelling by car, don't wear your jacket. Hang it up on a coat hanger so that it is not creased when you arrive for the interview.

PUNCTUALITY

This can be related to the above subject but is still just as important. Make sure you leave with plenty of time to spare before your interview. You're applying for a teaching post where punctuality is absolutely vital. It's far better to arrive an hour early than 5 minutes late! Ideally you should aim to arrive 30 minutes before the interview and sit in the car, re-read the job description for the role or information about the educational establishment you are applying to join.

THE TEACHER INTERVIEW FORMAT

Just by virtue of the fact you have been offered an interview indicates that the educational establishment believes you have the potential to work for them in that important role. They will have already carried out a screening process based during the initial application centred on the qualities and attributes relating to the teaching post that you have applied for. The interview is designed so that the employer can see you in person and look at your demeanour, presence, personality and appearance along with the opportunity to ask you questions based around your application form and your experiences of teaching thus far.

You may be competing against up to 6 applicants, so it is important that you stand out in a positive way and not for the wrong reasons. The basics of interview etiquette are key to your success and you need to prepare for these as much as you do the interview questions themselves.

Most teaching interviews will follow the following format:

INTRODUCTION AND ICEBREAKER

The interviewer should give you a brief overview of the interview process and possibly the role that you are applying for. You should be familiar with the job description and person specification prior to the interview so this will come as no surprise. Dependant on the interviewer, you will be given the opportunity to tell the panel about yourself. Your response should be prepared beforehand and you can use this as an opportunity to sell yourself. You should cover brief topics relating to your experience, qualifications, outside interests and ambitions. If you tell the panel that in your spare time you are working towards a qualification that relates to your progression in the teaching sector then this can only be a good thing. Try to keep your introduction as brief as possible and don't go over two minutes in length. Here's an example of an introduction you could use:

"Hello, my name is Antony Stagg and I have been working as a teacher for the past 5 years now. It is a job that I am very passionate about and I always take my work extremely seriously. Outside of work I am a dedicated family man who understands the need for stability. I am an organised person who works hard to achieve his goals. I have many hobbies including gardening, walking and reading. Within work I am both organised, professional, flexible and highly conscientious. My appraisals to date speak volumes of the work I am capable of delivering and I can assure you that, if I am successful in this post, I will work very hard to deliver the curriculum in a professional manner and surpass your expectations."

THE INTERVIEW ITSELF

This is the area in which you are asked a series of questions relating to your application form and the teaching post that you have applied for. This is where you should do most of the talking and if you have prepared well enough you will be able to answer most questions, although it is not unusual to find yourself struggling to answer one or two. In this situation it is always best not to waffle. If you really don't know the answer to a particular question then just say so. We will cover the key areas for research a little later on.

THE OPPORTUNITY TO ASK QUESTIONS

This is a time for you to ask some questions to the panel and it will usually come towards the end of the interview. You should usually have two or three questions that you want to ask at the end.

Make sure your questions are relevant but always avoid asking questions relating to leave or salary (unless you are specifically asked). Ask questions that relate to the role or development opportunities within the educational organisation. You may have researched the organisation and found that a new project is being developed or a new curriculum is being introduced. Ask them how the project is developing and what plans they have for the future. Don't ask questions where you are trying to be clever or questions

that are too technical. If you try to catch them out they won't be impressed and they may come back and ask you a similarly difficult question.

QUESTIONS TO ASK

> During my research I noticed that you have just launched a new pilot scheme aimed at delivering improved educational content to the students. Has it been successful? (This shows a caring attitude towards the school, and also that you've carried out your research.)

QUESTIONS TO AVOID

> How have I done during the interview? Have I passed? (This question demonstrates impatience and a slight level of arrogance. The interview panel will need to time to discuss your performance before making their decision.)

> How much leave will I get in this role? (I don't need to explain why this is a bad question!)

> How quickly can I progress in terms of promotion? (This question, whilst demonstrating a level of enthusiasm, shows the panel that you have little intention of staying in the role long.)

THE END OF THE INTERVIEW

Make sure you remain positive at this stage and thank the entire panel for their time. This is a good opportunity to shake their hands. If you do shake their hand then make sure it's a firm grip and look them in the eye.

At the end of every interview always leave the panel with a final statement. Here's an example:

"I just want to say thank you for inviting me along to interview. I've really enjoyed the experience and I have learnt a tremendous amount about the school. If I am successful then I promise you that I will work very hard in the role and I will do all that I can to surpass your expectations."

This statement is very powerful. This is the final thing the interview panel will remember you for. When you leave the interview room they are probably going to assess/discuss your performance. Just as first impressions last, so do final impressions also.

CHAPTER 2
A FORMULA
FOR SUCCESS

Over the next few pages and chapters I will provide you with a useful formula for success and more importantly how you can use it to assist you during every teaching interview that you attend. The formula itself is a simple one, and is broken down into three different sections:

- Interview technique
- Research
- Responding to the interview questions

I will explain in a manner that demonstrates how I would prepare for a teaching interview.

INTERVIEW TECHNIQUE

During my pre-interview preparation, I will concentrate on developing your interview technique. This will involve concentrating on the following key areas:

- Creating a positive first impression
- Presentation
- Effective communication
- Body language and posture

- Final questions
- Creating a positive final impression

Let's now break down each of these areas and look at them in detail.

CREATING A POSITIVE FIRST IMPRESSION

The teaching interview panel will naturally create a first impression of you. As soon as you walk into the interview room they will be forming an opinion. Therefore, it is important that you get off on the right foot. As a teacher you will be a role model for the educational establishment and the panel will be assessing you from the word go. Whenever I walk into any interview room I will always follow this process:

Knock before I enter the room

Walk into the interview room standing tall and smiling

Stand by the interview chair and say
"Hello, I'm Richard, pleased to meet you."

Shake the hand of each interviewer firmly, whilst looking them in the eye

Sit down in the interview chair, only when invited to do so

By following the above process you will be creating a positive first impression and demonstrating good qualities such as manners, self-discipline, politeness, motivation and an ability to present a good image to your students.

PRESENTATION

Presentation effectively means how I intend to dress for the interview and also how I intend to come across. I want the interview panel to see me as a professional, motivated, conscientious and caring person who is taking the interview very seriously.

For the interview I will make sure that my suit is cleaned and pressed, my shoes are polished, and my personal hygiene is up to standard. This means simple things such as taking a shower, shaving, having a haircut and

general grooming. I will always avoid brightly coloured clothes and generally go for a conservative approach such a dark blue, black or grey suit. If I do decide to wear any brighter, more vibrant colours, then this will be in form of a tie. I would strongly advise that you avoid brightly coloured socks or ties with cartoon characters on them!

As I have previously mentioned within this guide, you may decide to wear subtle colours that match the branding of the educational establishment you are being interviewed for. This is a good way of demonstrating a commitment to the school before you even join.

Let me know explain the difference between a good applicant and a poor one.

A GOOD APPLICANT

A good applicant is someone who has taken the time to prepare fully for the teaching interview. They will have researched both the educational organisation they are applying to join and also the teaching role that they are being interviewed for. They may not know every detail about the school, college or university but it will be clear that they have made an effort to find out important facts and information.

They will be well presented at the interview and they will be confident, but not overconfident. As soon as they walk into the interview room they will be polite and courteous and they will sit down in the interview chair only when invited to do so. Throughout the interview they will sit upright in the chair and communicate in a positive manner. They will be aware that communication is an important part of the teaching role and they will have worked hard on this area in the build up to interview. If they do not know the answer to a question they will say so and they won't try to waffle. At the end of the interview they will ask positive questions about the school and the role before shaking hands and leaving.

A POOR APPLICANT

A poor applicant could be any combination of the following. They will be late for the interview or even forget to turn up at all. They will have made little effort to dress smartly and they will have carried out little or no preparation. When asked questions about the role they will have little or no knowledge. Throughout the interview they will appear to be unenthusiastic about the whole process and will look as if they want the interview to be over as soon as possible. Whilst sat in the interview chair they will slouch and fidget. At the end of the interview they will try to ask clever questions that are intended to impress the panel.

IMPROVING INTERVIEW TECHNIQUE

How you present yourself during the interview is important. The interviewers will not only assess your responses to the interview questions but they will also pay attention to the way you present yourself. Don't forget, teachers are role models for the school. A candidate could give excellent responses to the interview questions but if they present themselves in a negative manner then this can lose them marks.

Take a look at the following diagrams, which indicate both poor technique and good technique.

Poor interview technique
The candidate appears to be too relaxed and casual for an interview.

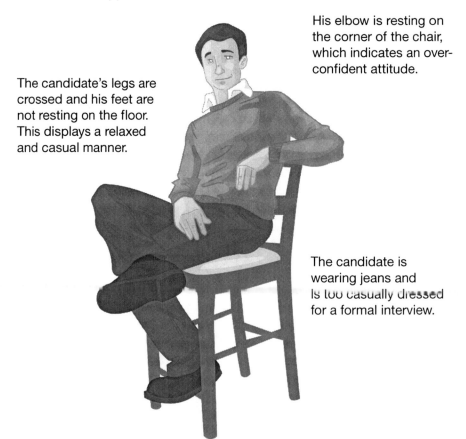

His elbow is resting on the corner of the chair, which indicates an over-confident attitude.

The candidate's legs are crossed and his feet are not resting on the floor. This displays a relaxed and casual manner.

The candidate is wearing jeans and Is too casually dressed for a formal interview.

Good interview technique

The candidate is smiling and he portrays a confident, but not over-confident manner.

The candidate is dressed wearing a smart suit. It is clear that he has made an effort in his presentation.

His hands are in a stable position, which will prevent him from fidgeting. He could also place his hands palms facing downwards and resting on his knees.

He is sitting upright in the interview chair with his feet resting on the floor. He is not slouching and he portrays himself in a positive manner.

In the build up to your interview practise a number of mock interviews. Look to improve your interview technique as well as working on your responses to the interview questions. A great way to do this is practise with friends, someone who will take it seriously and support you. Alternatively use a video camera, or a built in camera on a laptop. This allows you to record and play back your responses so you can see how you are answering questions, it also helps you see improvements in body language and general confidence. Remember, the more you practise, the more you will relieve the anxiety you will naturally feel.

Female interview technique

The candidate is smiling and she portrays a confident, professional manner.

She is sitting upright in the interview chair with her feet resting on the floor. She is not slouching and portrays herself in a positive manner.

EFFECTIVE COMMUNICATION

How you communicate is obviously very important in the role of a teacher. If you are a poor communicator then there is no way you will be employed by the educational establishment.

Effective communication is all about how you speak to the interview panel, and also how you listen to what they have to say.

When responding to the interview questions you should speak clearly and concisely, avoiding all forms of waffle, slang or hesitations such as 'erm'. Look at each interview panel member when answering each question. Even though an interview question will be asked by one member of the panel at a time, you should always respond to the entire panel collectively. Look them in they eyes when speaking to them but never stare them out. This will only portray you in an aggressive or confrontational manner.

If you are unsure about a response to an interview question then just be honest.

Then say you don't know the answer, and explain what steps you will to get the correct answer. For example if their was a gap in your subject knowledge there will be resources you can access, training courses you could go on, or finding more experienced member of staff who would be able to point you in the right direction. The important thing here is demonstrating the hunger and motivation to find out, as there are always questions we don't know the answer to. The temptation however is to try and answer, but all you will do is waffle and make the situation worse.

When the interview panel are speaking to me, or if they are asking me a question, I will always demonstrate good listening skills. This means that I will use facial expressions to show that I am taking onboard what they are saying and I will also nod to show them that I understand the question(s).

BODY LANGUAGE AND POSTURE

Whilst sat in the interview I will always make a conscious effort to sit upright and not slouch in the chair. I personally like to use my hands to emphasise points when responding to the questions but I will be careful not to overdo it. Even if the interview is going great and you are building up a good rapport with the panel, don't let your standards drop. Always maintain good body language and posture for the duration of the interview.

FINAL QUESTIONS

Before I attend the interview I will always think of two questions to ask the panel at the end. However, don't be trapped in the thinking that you must ask questions. It is acceptable to say:

"Thank you but I don't have any questions. I have already carried out lots of research relating to the role, the school and the curriculum and you have answered my questions during the interview."

Some people believe that you must ask three, four or even five questions at the end of the interview – this is total nonsense. Remember that the interview panel will have other people to interview and they will also need time to discuss your performance.

If you do decide to ask questions then make sure they are relevant.

CREATING A POSITIVE FINAL IMPRESSION

I have already discussed this during a previous section. I believe that a final positive statement can work wonders:

"I just want to say thank you for inviting me along to interview. I've really enjoyed the experience and I have learnt a tremendous amount about your college. If I am successful then I promise you that I will work very hard in the role and I will do all that I can to surpass your expectations."

RESEARCHING THE TEACHER ROLE AND THE EDUCATIONAL ESTABLISHMENT

I highly recommend you try to visit the school or college you are applying to join before you attend the interview. This serves a number of purposes but the most important are demonstrating commitment and dedication to the potential employer but also assisting you in your preparation for the interview.

Other great ways to find out about a school are by visiting their website, if they have one. Look for their 'mission statement', 'goals or 'values' and try to learn as much about the curriculum as possible. Another effective research method is to type the schools name into a search engine such as Google or Yahoo. This should bring up a number of links for you to research.

Make sure that the information you read is current and up to date, and don't

waste time reading items that are more than a year old as you will most probably find that they have changed since then.

TOPICS YOU SHOULD RESEARCH

You can spend many weeks studying different topics, but the following areas should be a priority in your research plan:

- Do they offer any development programmes for their teachers?
- When was the school established?
- Is it a large school and do they have overseas interests?
- Where do their students come from?
- Who is the Head teacher?
- Has the school been successful and what are the recent Ofsted reports saying? Can you suggest any areas for improvement?
- What are their short, medium and long term goals?
- What are their values and policies of the school?
- What is unique about the school?
- Has the school had any success stories of late?
- What are the strengths of the school?

TOP TIP: Only research things that are relevant and don't waste time reading irrelevant articles. Look to see if the school has a magazine or newsletter. Check out league tables and find out about the academic achievements, use your time wisely. Look at what awards they have won!

RESPONDING TO THE INTERVIEW QUESTIONS

The majority of teaching interviews will contain two different types of questions. There will normally be motivational questions and situational questions. Here's an explanation as to how they differ.

MOTIVATIONAL QUESTIONS

Motivation interview questions are questions that are designed to assess the reasons why you want the job, what you have to offer, how much research you have done and also why you are the best candidate for the job. Whilst they are relatively easy to prepare for, you should still spend plenty of time getting your responses ready to the perceived motivational interview questions as these can, and often do, catch people out. Here's a list of sample motivational interview questions.

Q. Tell us about yourself.

Q. Talk me through your CV.

Q. Why do you want this job?

Q. What do you have to offer?

Q. What skills do you have that would be of benefit in this role?

Q. Why should we give you the job and not the next candidate?

Q. I don't think you're experienced enough for this job. Convince me otherwise.

Q. What have you done to find out about this school and the role that you are applying for?

Q. How do you define success?

Q. What will you do if you are unsuccessful today?

You will see from the above list that the questions are very much aimed at your 'motivation' for wanting to join their educational establishment. Before you attend the interview I would suggest that you prepare responses for all of the above questions, many of which we will cover later in this book.

SITUATIONAL QUESTIONS

Situational interview questions are slightly harder to respond to. In order to determine the type of situational interview question you could be asked, I would recommend that you get a copy of the person specification or job description for the role. Once you have this to hand, you will then be able to prepare responses to the type of situations that you will be expected to perform within the role. The key to scoring high during your responses to this type of questioning is to provide evidence of where you have already been in this type of situation.

The following list of situational interview questions are ones that I recommend you prepare for.

Q. Give an example of where you have worked as part of a team to achieve a difficult goal or task.

Q. Give an example of where you have provided innovative teaching to a class or a student.

Q. Give an example of where you have dealt with an unhappy parent who is complaining about their child's progress at school.

Q. Give an example of where you have challenged a pupil's behaviour that was unacceptable or against school policy.

Q. Give an example of where you have made a difficult decision despite objection from other people.

Q. Give an example of where you have taken on board constructive criticism during an appraisal.

Q. Give an example of where you have dealt with a difficult or aggressive pupil.

Q. Give an example of where you have resolved an issue with a work colleague.

CAR METHOD

The CAR method is one that I have used during my preparation for many interviews in the past. It works most effectively when preparing responses to situational type interview questions. I would certainly recommend that you try using it.

The CAR method basically ensures that your responses to the interview questions follow a concise logical sequence and also that you cover every possible area. Here's a break down of what it actually means:

CONTEXT, which means background. Where were you working? Who were you with? What was the challenge or task?

ACTION, I will then move on and explain what action I specifically took, and also what action other people took. Did you consult with someone? Did you do something creative? What is it you did?

RESULT, I will finally explain what the result was following my actions. It is important to make sure that the result was positive as a result of your actions.

Have a go at using the CAR method when creating responses to interview questions. Write down the question at the top of a sheet of paper and write down each individual element underneath it.

An example is Question 33 Can you tell us about a situation when you have had to work under pressure?

C - *"With my previous school I was in charge of the mock interview process for our YR10 students, which takes considerable organisation with administration staff, students, other teaching staff, caretakers, and of course employers.*

I led a team to organise the whole day and we all had responsibilities but on the morning of the event, one of the administrators was ill, which meant we can no contact point for employers on the morning, or somebody to meet and greet and ensure they receive a positive experience of the school.

A - *With only a couple of hours before the arrival of the employers we were stretched, so I spoke to the Deputy Head Teacher about bringing in a couple of Yr13 students to help support the event.*

After this was agreed I spent time with the 2 students to explain what was required, the objectives and to give them a crash course in handling customers as well as encouragement as they were nervous.

R - *During and after the event employers commented on the professionalism of the event, and also particularly the two students who helped support at short notice. The skills demonstrated, such as creating a positive first impression, communicating clearly and precisely won one of the students a part time job with an employer. So from a extremely pressurised situation, by working as a team, placing trust in our students, we turned a negative position into a positive and further cemented relationships with the business community."*

Many things go through our minds when we are in interviews because we are nervous. Use CAR as a logical structure to organise your thoughts when answering situational questions. Remember the interview panel will want examples and depth to your answers!

CHAPTER 3
SAMPLE INTERVIEW QUESTIONS & RESPONSES

Within this section of the guide I will provide you with lots of sample teacher interview questions. Following the many of questions you will be provided you with a sample response to help guide you in the right direction. I have also provided you with a blank template following many of the questions, which I suggest you use to create your own response to each question. This will make sure that you cover every eventuality, and it will also prepare you far more effectively for your forthcoming teaching interview.

WARM-UP QUESTIONS

These types of questions are usually asked at the beginning of an interview. They are sometimes used by an interview panel to give you the opportunity to warm up in preparation for the assessable questions.

Q. How was your journey here today?

This question is very easy to answer. However, avoid single word or short replies such as:

"Yes it was good thanks."

Try to add more substance to your response and use it as an opportunity to talk to the panel and also show them that you have some great qualities such as organisation and preparation, key qualities of a teacher!

"Yes it was a good journey thanks. I've been to this college before during my research so I knew where to go. The last thing I wanted was to be late for the interview so I made sure that I arrived with plenty of time to spare."

Q. Why have you decided to apply for this particular teaching post?

This again is a very common interview question and one that needs to be answered carefully. Remember that an interview panel will have heard all of the usual responses such as *"I've wanted to work in a teaching role since I was a child"*, and *"This job just really appeals to me"*. These types of standard responses will gain you few marks.

It is crucial that you provide a response to this type of question that is unique, truthful and different to all of the other candidates.

Consider the following points:

Provide a response that demonstrates you've carried out plenty of research. During your research something has caught your eye about the job that is very appealing. It might be that you are passionate about helping students and pupils to get the most from their talents and you believe you have the skills to nurture those qualities. It may be that you have a natural gift for teaching and you also enjoy working under time constraints or pressure. This will demonstrate to the panel that you have looked into the role carefully and that you are fully aware of the tough requirements for the role. Remember that most candidates will apply for many different teaching jobs all at one time, and as a result they will fail to carry out any meaningful research. You, however, will be different.

Consider providing a response that demonstrates you have the key skills required to perform the teaching job competently. An example would be:

"I understand that this role requires excellent communication skills in order to get the most from the pupils. I believe I am very strong in this area and therefore I would be a valuable asset to the teaching team.

Having researched the job and school extensively I have noticed a common theme appearing time and time again – professionalism. I have also spoken to people who already work within this school, and the feedback I have received has been excellent. I really want to work for this school and the skills and experience I have already gained will allow me to contribute towards the school's goals in a positive manner."

Warm-up questions can come in any format. The main aim for you is to make sure that you speak and communicate with the panel. Always avoid single word answers or short responses. The easy questions are your opportunity to get warmed up, and they are also your chance to create a rapport with the interviewer panel.

We will now take a look at a number of main interview questions.

Question 1 – Tell me about yourself?

This is a common introductory question that many interviewers use to break the ice. It is designed to get you talking about something you know – You!

A big mistake usually made by the majority of people is that they predominantly focus on their family, children, hobbies or home life. Whilst you may have some interesting facts about your personal life you should either avoid these, unless specifically asked, or keep them very brief. Try to answer this type of question based around your own personal achievements, educational background, qualities that are relevant to the role and any on-going studies. It is good to say that you are motivated or enthusiastic but you MUST ensure that you provide examples or scenarios where this has been proven. For example you might say, *"I am a motivated person – whilst working for my previous school I achieved 'XYZ', which enabled them to achieve its goal in relation to an excellent Ofsted report."*

Giving specific, brief examples is positive. Remember that anyone can tell an interview panel that they are 'motivated', 'enthusiastic' or 'determined' but not everybody can prove it. Try to think about and use some of the following key words when structuring some of your answers:

- Motivated
- Flexible
- Professional
- Adaptable

- Self-starter

- Responsible

- Enthusiastic

- Dedicated

- Committed

- Reliable

- Trustworthy

- Initiative

- Team player

- Organised

- Focused

It is also a good idea to think of occasions where you have initiated projects or ideas at work, which have gone on to achieve results. This might be where you have demonstrated a new and innovative teaching method.

There now follows a sample response to this question. Once you have read it, use the template on the following page to create your own, based on your own individual situation:

"My strong points are that I am focused, enthusiastic and dedicated to the school that I am working for. For example, whilst working for my current school, I was able to contribute to improving the overall A-C GCSE grades of my Year 11 class for Maths by 25%, something of which I am very proud of.

I like to ensure that I maintain a healthy balance between my personal and professional life. This helps me to maintain a high level of performance at work. I am extremely organised at work and make sure that I plan my teaching day the night before at the very least. Where possible, I like to plan a few weeks in advance. This ensures that the students achieve the most effective teaching methods possible.

I also recently embarked on a Diploma course, which I am now halfway through. I enjoy new challenges and like to take care of my own self-development. I am an active person and enjoy visiting the gym 4 times a week. Some of my other hobbies include art, walking and cooking. I am a caring person and when I have the spare time I try to get involved in community events in my local town. I recently ran a half marathon raising £450 for a

local charity. I also noticed during my research that the school encourages its students to participate in raising money for charity. This is something that is close to my heart and, if successful, I would very much like to get involved in these activities.

Overall I would say that I am a reliable, self-conscious and hard-working person who always looks for ways to improve."

_____

TOP TIP: Take any literature or evidence that you have along with you to the interview to prove to the panel that you are genuine. It could be references, letters from parents, or awards etc.

_____

QUESTION 1

Tell me about yourself?

Question 2 – What have you learnt about this school?

This question is extremely common during teaching job interviews. It is designed to whittle out those candidates who apply for lots of teaching jobs at once. The employer will naturally only want to employ people who have genuine reasons for wanting to join their school. Anyone who is applying for lots of jobs with many different establishments is unlikely to stay for a prolonged period of time.

I would personally expect an interviewee to have researched the school thoroughly before they come to interview. If you take onboard my advice in the earlier pages of this guide then you will be able to answer this question with relative ease. Try to state what the ethos of the school is. Understand the vision and expectations of the school and know internal information on the size, structure and organisation. You should also be aware of the wider political issues in relation to recent Ofsted reports, issues facing the school and its relationship with the local community.

Your research is paramount to your success and shows that you haven't just turned up on the day to make the numbers up. By learning all you can about the school you will demonstrate a commitment before you have begun working for them.

Sample response to question 2

"In the build up to the interview I carried out lots of research about your school. I found out that there are 80 staff who work in various roles, from teachers, teaching assistants, administrative workers, caretakers, cleaners and canteen staff; all of which carry out a very important role in maintaining the high standards the school sets itself. The school has a very good reputation for delivering high quality teaching, and as a result, has received excellent Ofsted reports, something which the school and its staff must be very proud of. It has also received Investors in People status. During my research I was impressed to note that the Ofsted report praised the school for its high standards. Staff are committed to raising the aspirations and achievements so that the students can reach their potential. The school has also achieved its ambition of increasing the pass rate in exams and the GCSE English and Mathematics examination results in 2011 were the highest the school has achieved to date. The proportion of students gaining five or more GCSEs at grades A*-C is now well above the national average, as is also the proportion of students gaining higher grades.

It is obvious that the school only employs committed and dedicated people who can bring something positive to the working environment and I believe I can fulfil this role. I want to work in a school that has high standards and I believe my teaching style will help the school further its aspirations and goals.

I am a professional and skilled person who would love to work in a school like yours, which constantly strives to improve and deliver excellence."

Now use the template on the following page to construct a response based on your research and centred on the company you are applying to join.

QUESTION 2
What have you learnt about this school?

Question 3 – Teaching requires a high degree of flexibility. Would you say that you are a flexible person?

This question is designed to see if you are flexible in relation to working hours and also your level of commitment as a teacher? As a teacher you will be required to work outside of normal working hours and be expected to mark and assess your students' work.

The obvious and most appropriate answer to this question would be 'Yes'. It is then best to follow your answer up with evidence that you are flexible. Provide details of where you have already been flexible in another teaching role if possible. If this is your first teaching post then provide an alternative example.

There now follows a sample response to this question. Once you have read it, use the template on the following page to create your own, based on your own individual situation:

"Yes I am very flexible and I fully understand that the role will require me to be available when required. In my previous teaching role I fully under-stood that I would be required to work outside of normal teaching hours. I would usually set aside a few hours at the weekend to catch up on any marking and assessing and I would never let my work fall over into the following week. I believe that I am very flexible and again in previous role I was involved in co-ordinating and managing the Year 9 school football team, which meant regular commitment on a Saturday morning as well as arranging tours in the half term holidays."

QUESTION 3

Teaching requires a high degree of flexibility. Would you say that you are a flexible person?

Question 4 – What are your strengths?

This is an extremely common interview question and one that you must prepare for. When answering this type of question I would advise that you give work-related examples. You should try to think of at least three good strengths that you possess, and provide an example of when you have used those strengths.

You may be able to give an answer along the following lines:

"One of my strengths is that I have the ability to implement change in dif-
ficult circumstances. For example whilst working for my previous employer
I implemented a new curriculum under difficult and adverse conditions. I
managed to introduce it into the classroom in a positive manner and all of
the students responded positively towards it. The end result was that the
majority of my students achieved pass grades of A* -C in their GCSE ex-
amination. I have the ability to understand that the needs of the school will
always come first. My strengths include an ability to inspire and motivate a
classroom."

This type of answer demonstrates to the panel that you are able to prove your strengths as opposed to just saying that you have them. Anyone can say that they are motivated, enthusiastic, dedicated or reliable, but proving that you have those strengths is a different matter.

Being able to demonstrate that you have strengths with solid evidence will give you higher scores.

Use the template on the following page to create your own response, based on your own individual strengths.

QUESTION 4

What are your strengths?

Question 5 - Tell us about your experiences working with students of different ages.

The question is asking for you to provide details of your experiences; therefore, you should provide this. In your response try to explain how you are aware that each age group of student will have different needs and therefore a different teaching styles and approaches will be required. Provide details of how you have maintained the enthusiasm and concentration levels of different groups of students.

"During my time as a teacher I have been involved with Years 5 and 6 as I led the primary liaison within my previous school to great effect. This role enabled me to build relationships with head teachers and understand the curriculum in more detail at primary level. By doing this I could use my creativity to plan activities that would engage students and help support their development. As result of engaging the primary schools, their teachers, and also inviting parents in to see what we were doing with the students, we saw an increase in student numbers for our intake into year 7 up by 34 places from the previous year.

I have also been involved with Years 12 and 13 in supporting apprenticeships. Much of this has stemmed from a passion to help with the career direction for our older students and ensuring they go through an interview process with members of staff and employers we have relationships with to determine which is the best pathway for that student.

By ensuring students know what is available to them and being flexible with our curriculum I was then able to work with other members of staff to develop our own apprenticeship scheme with local employers and ensure the best possible learning experience for our students.

Obviously when working with any age group it is important to customise the learning experience, understand the curriculum and aim to maximise the opportunities for all students."

QUESTION 5

Tell us about your experiences working with students of different ages.

Question 6 - Describe your teaching style?

When responding to the question however try and demonstrate that you are:

- passionate about teaching
- passionate about the students achieving high grades
- passionate about making the classroom experience both informative, interesting and memorable

If you don't have a lot of teaching experience, then try to think about the great teachers you've had and what made them so effective. What did they do that inspired you to spend so many years learning your trade? Another useful tip is to think about what you don't like in a teacher. Reflecting on what you don't like can give you insights about what you do like, and that can help you to define your own teaching philosophy. Finally, remember that teaching is about the student!

QUESTION 6

Describe your teaching style?

Question 7 - Why do you want to become a teacher?

Only you will know the answer to this question but you may decide to include some or all of the following reasons in your response:

- An ability to make a difference to someone's life.
- Being empowered to lay good foundations for a student so that they can go on to achieve great things.
- The high level of responsibility that comes with such a role.
- The sense of achievement knowing that you have contributed to a student's success in their examinations.
- Being a positive role model

"I wanted to become a teacher because of my desire to make a difference to young people. My biggest motivational factor for working is the sense of achievement by applying myself to help others. An example of this was in my first year of teaching I introduced new additional classes after school to help students of all abilities in my Year 9 IT class. I worked in a inter city school were many parents worked until after 4pm and had relatively few childcare options. Recognising the opportunity to support not only the parents and build a working relationship with them, it was an opportunity to help students with homework in IT, in which I provided incentives for them to stay behind such as HMV vouchers and MP3 players that I would buy and use as reward at the end of the half term. This encouraged attendance, motivation and work ethic. It is this passion in wanting to become a teacher and going the extra mile that resulted in grades increasing, relationships developing and me feeling an enormous amount of satisfaction!"

QUESTION 7

Why do you want to become a teacher?

Question 8 – What are your weaknesses?

Possibly the worst answer you can give for a question of this nature is that you don't have any weaknesses. Being able to identify that you have weaknesses is a strength in itself. Obviously it is important that you answer this question carefully as you could reduce your chances of success if you portray yourself in a negative light. For example, if you state that you are not a good communicator or you are disorganised then you're probably not the right person for the job!

Here's an example of a response to this type of question:

"In my previous job I found it difficult to delegate work to others. I can be a bit of a perfectionist at times and I like a job or task to be done correctly to a high standard. Unfortunately this lack of trust caused problems within my team and a member of staff approached me to tell me they were not happy with the way I was working. I took their comments onboard and decided to ask the rest of the team if they felt the same. The feedback I received was along the same lines – that the majority of people felt I should delegate more work and responsibility to them. Following this feedback I decided to change my style of approach and began to delegate more work, plac- ing greater trust in my colleagues. This had a very positive effect and the workload increased dramatically as a result of this change. Morale within the team improved too and now I hold regular feedback meetings with my colleagues to see how we can improve."

This type of response identifies that you have a weakness, but also identi- fies a number of strengths. It shows that you have the ability to look at yourself and make changes where needed. Accepting constructive criti- cism is one thing, but doing something about it is another. This also leads on to another possible 'strength' quality in the fact that you can identify your weaknesses and do something about them.

Use the template on the following page to create your own answer to this question based on your own individual weaknesses.

QUESTION 8

What are your weaknesses?

Question 9 – Do you enjoy working as part of a team?

The answer to this type of question depends on the type of teaching job you are applying for. If you are applying for a teaching position in a large school then obviously you need to answer this in a manner that shows you are a team player. Conversely if you are applying for a position that involves a lot of 'lone working' then it is a good idea to say that you feel comfortable working on your own. Possibly the best answer for this type of question is to state that you are adaptable and can work in any educational environment. Again, if you can give examples of situations where you have been an effective team member or achieved results independently then this is far better. Although you will be responsible for teaching on your own the majority of the time, you will still be required to work as a team to assist the educational establishment in achieving its targets. Being a team player is very much an important aspect of a teacher's role.

"At university, during my placement at a local primary school, I enjoyed working as part of a team as I knew that I could benefit from the huge amount of experience and expertise from working with so many teachers. What I brought to the team was new ideas, willingness to learn, and hard work in supporting other colleagues in developing resources and lessons. In return I gained mentorship from two teachers with I still retain today. By sharing ideas in working in a team this always helps with the fundamental reason for being in teaching, which is to help students reach their maximum potential. I am however comfortable working by myself as much of what I do is in the classroom. I relish the challenge and opportunity this brings in helping make our students the best they can be."

Use the template on the following page to create your own answer to this question based on your own experiences.

QUESTION 9

Do you enjoy working in a team environment?

Question 10 – In what ways would you encourage creativity in your classroom?

Creative teaching is essential to maintaining your students' concentration levels. As a teacher you will have to come up with new and innovative ways to maintain your students' concentration. Take a look at the following sample response to this question.

"Creativity is the most important aspect of teaching. It allows students to learn in a fun environment, where they can become active and engaged and retain the information delivered more easily. Being creative means working with learning mentors getting new input from them, changing the physical class environment, and using technology, games, and encouraging teamwork.

During my last role teaching geography, I used a combination of Google maps and Google earth to show students in more detail different towns, rivers, glaciers and landmarks. Students were given the task of planning a geography field trip to Germany plotting different routes, and presenting back to the class why they choose that route. We also sought help from employers, in particular with one lesson we used video conferencing to link for students to understand the different careers available by studying geography, this was something that had not been done before in the school. It was a fantastic experience for students to interact with employers using innovative technology.

It is essential to involve the students in every aspect of my teaching. This would ensure their concentration levels were maintained. If students enjoy the lesson, they are far more likely to achieve higher grades.

I also involve the students by continually asking them questions about the information I was passing on to them. I would create a short quiz at the end of each lesson to assess the student's levels of attention. I would ask the students to work in small groups and come up with exciting and fun projects for them to participate in. Creativity in the classroom is essential, but none of this would be possible without a passionate teacher. I believe my passion comes across in abundance during my lessons and the students will certainly gain from this."

Now use the template on the following page to create your own answer to this question based on your own opinions and beliefs.

QUESTION 10

In what ways would you encourage creativity in your classroom?

Question 11 – What are you like at time management?

Time management is undoubtedly a skill not everyone possesses. Being able to manage your time effectively is not easy but it is an essential part of the teacher's role. When you get into work, do you already know what you are going to achieve by the end of the day? During the final 30 minutes of your working day do you plan the following day's activities and tasks in order of priority? Do you keep a list of important objectives and tasks and cross them off when they are completed? If you are teaching do you keep irrelevant discussion to an absolute minimum and always ensure you finish on time? Are you acutely aware of others' valuable time as well as your own, and do you make certain that time is not wasted unnecessarily by going over into another teachers lesson time?

Your time management is essential to the success of the curriculum. The above information gives you a number of time management tools to use when constructing your answer. It is also important to remember to emphasise that you are flexible with your time when needed, and that you reorganise your workload in order to meet specific important deadlines.

"I am very effective at time management. I am the type of person who is extremely organised and knows what they want to achieve during each day. I like to keep lists, which act as a reminder of what I want to achieve and in what timeframe. For example, if I have a busy teaching schedule planned for the forthcoming week, I will always write down what I want to do during that week, the week before, including my lesson plans. This allows me to plan ahead and also makes sure that I have everything in place so that I can achieve each objective. I fully understand that the role I am applying for will require me to be competent at time management, and I am fully prepared for this."

Now use the template on the following page to create your own answer to this question based on your own skills, qualities and experience.

QUESTION 11

What are you like at time management?

Question 12 – What are you like at taking criticism from a senior teacher or Head Teacher?

Regardless of how you think you would react, it is important to tell the interview panel that you look at this in a positive manner. Of course you do not want to portray an image that you are a pushover, but an answer along the following lines would be acceptable:

"Whilst working for my current school, a situation arose where I was criticised for a mistake. At the time of the criticism I felt disappointed in my own performance, but knew it was important to learn from my mistake and improve for next time. I understand that not everybody is perfect and when we make mistakes it is the ability to move on and improve for next time that is important. I spoke with my head teacher after the mistake was made, apologised and made certain I improved my performance in that particular area."

The above type of response identifies that you have the ability to accept criticism but also that you are sensitive to it too. Nobody likes criticism of any kind but in this response you have shown that you did not get angry, defensive or arrogant but instead you turned a negative situation into a positive one.

Now use the template on the following page to create your own answer to this question based on your own skills, qualities and experience. Try to think of a situation where you made a mistake, and provide an example of what you did to improve. When constructing your response try to include words such as 'reflect' and 'evaluate'. If you have not previously worked in a teaching role then use an alternative work related example.

QUESTION 12

What are you like at taking criticism from a senior teacher or Head Teacher?

Before we move on to the next set of interview questions and answers, take a look at the following teacher interview questions followed by some important tips on how to respond to them.

Question 13 - *What do you do to prepare your students for their mock exams?*

Focus on revision techniques and how to adapt to exam conditions. Mention techniques such as mind maps and other useful ways to revise. You also need to show knowledge of assessment for learning as this would be a big focus in teaching and would need to form part of your answer.

You may then wish to say that you give your students a series of mini tests and exams in the build up to their mocks in order to clarify that the lesson plans are effective, and that they are absorbing the information you are providing them with. It is important to evaluate your teaching with your students and this is a good way to achieve it.

QUESTION 13

What do you do to prepare your students for their mock exams?

Question 14 - What would you do if a student revealed sensitive information to you that clearly placed them in an at risk situation?

This situation must always be referred to the child protection officer at the school. Do not attempt to deal with the situation on your own. Follow a stepped approach and deal with this issue in accordance with the schools policies on child protection and sensitive information. Make sure you have asked for a copy of the schools policies and procedures prior to the interview.

"Whilst working in my previous school I was approached by one of my students who was having difficulties at home, this involved a sensitive situation which involved his parents and the Police. It was clear by him revealing this information to me personally that he was in a lot of danger.

The first step was to contact the safeguarding officer in the school who took responsibility for the case and involved further trained staff from the local authority. By following the school policy I was ensuring that he received the best possible care so his future would not be jeopardised.

As a result of following the procedure the trained professionals were able to work with both the school and the family to put a programme together which involved constant monitoring of his progress. This enabled him to live a relatively normal life, which in turn made him more comfortable in school."

QUESTION 14

What would you do if a student revealed sensitive information to you that clearly placed them in an at risk situation?

Question 15 - How do you measure student performance in your classroom?

You need to demonstrate in answering this question that you can use data and strategies such as the Fischer Family Trust system and the Assessment for Learning Strategy to evaluate student performance. You may also wish to set extension work, test and quiz questions to follow up learning.

Prior to delivering a sample lesson, you will know which age group and subject area you will be teaching. This gives you the opportunity to revise and demonstrate your subject knowledge.

Remember – if you need more information, do not be afraid to ask for it!

QUESTION 15

How do you measure student performance in your classroom?

Question 16 - How would you ensure that you could demonstrate subject knowledge in your lesson?

If you had researched the qualifications the school offers or expects you to teach you will always be able to answer this question. Do your research and revise!

Always look for every opportunity to demonstrate subject knowledge in your lesson plan and throughout your interview.

QUESTION 16

How would you ensure that you could demonstrate subject knowledge in your lesson?

Question 17 – What would you do if you witnessed a pupil being bullied at school?

There is only one correct answer to this type of question, and that is you must intervene and take action to stop it from occurring. Make sure you say that you would follow school policy and always try to be sensitive to the needs of the person who is being bullied. You would probably need to take the time to talk to the person who is on the receiving end of such behaviour, and support/comfort them. Dependant on their wishes, you would consider informing their parents. You would also need to tackle the student or pupil who was carrying out the bullying. They would need educating in order to prevent this kind of destructive behaviour from happening again in the future.

It is important to say to the interviewer that you would read the schools policy on bullying and harassment before you joined the team. If you can obtain of copy of this before the interview, then it is good practice to read it. Always remember that this type of behaviour is not tolerated, both in society, in schools and in employment. The employer has a responsibility under law to prevent such behaviour. To read more guidance about how to deal with bullying and harassment in the workplace, please visit:

www.direct.gov.uk

www.bullying.co.uk

www.nspcc.org.uk

"To begin with, I would certainly take some form of action to stop it from happening. This would be in-line with the schools policy, which I am familiar with already. Bullying or harassment should never be tolerated at school or in the workplace. I would make sure that I am conversant with the policy before taking action. I would do all that I could to stop the inappropriate behaviour, and that might involve informing the parents of the student who was carrying out the bullying. I would speak to the person who was being bullied or harassed and do all that I could to support them. Sometimes those people who are acting as the bully do not realise what they are doing and the impact of their actions. Therefore it is important to challenge the person who is carrying out the inappropriate behaviour."

Now use the template that follows to create your own answer to this question.

QUESTION 17

What would you do if you witnessed a pupil being bullied at school?

Question 18 – What would you do if a student wasn't handing her homework on a regular basis?

The most important thing is to get to the root of the problem as soon as possible to prevent it from becoming a bigger problem. In incidents of this nature there is normally an external factor that is preventing the student from handing in their homework in on time. You should be sensitive to wards the student and ask in a caring manner whether there are any issues affecting their ability to hand in their homework. They may be struggling with the work, have become de-motivated or are having problems at home.

Now use the template that follows to construct your own response to this question.

QUESTION 18

What would you do if a student wasn't handing her homework on a regular basis?

Question 19 – *Where do you see yourself in five years time?*

This is an extremely common question amongst interview panels. Be careful how you answer this one though. I have been on interview panels where people say 'I don't know I'll see what happens.' This is not a very good response to this question and displays a lack of ambition and drive.

I have also been on interview panels where people have given responses such as:

"I want to be sat in your seat doing your job."

Whilst I don't disbelieve them I feel that this type of response displays arrogance rather than confidence.

Try to structure your answer in a way that shows you are positive about the future and that you are committed to developing in the role of a teacher within their educational establishment. Most head teachers want you to show that you have aspirations and a willingness to progress. There is nothing wrong with saying that you have ambition - for example you may have a 5 year plan to be Head of Department.

You may also be asked as part of this question *"How are you going to get there?"*

Again, be honest! Show that you are ambitious and willing to take extra responsibility on for free. Show that you are willing to shadow your head of department and work closely with senior colleagues to know what the job is all about.

A good answer to use might be along the following lines:

"I believe I am the right person for this job. If successful I would like to further develop my skills and knowledge by initially learning all I can about the role and the school. If successful I intend to stay with this school for many years. In five years' time I would want to be settled in to role and have my students achieving the highest grades possible. I would also want to be helping the school achieve excellent results in its Ofsted reports. Above all I will be looking to have developed both personally and professionally during that time."

Now use the template on the following page to create your own answer to this question. When creating your response, try to display a level of ambition, drive and a desire to personally and professionally improve.

QUESTION 19

Where do you see yourself in five years time?

Question 20 – What are your classroom rules? How do you make students familiar with the rules?

As a teacher you will be responsible for setting your own standards in the classroom. The school will have its own code of conduct which you should use as a basis for classroom discipline. Consider the following classroom rules and use them to create your own response to this question:

- Arrive on time, with the necessary books and equipment.
- Enter the classroom quietly and prepare to start work immediately.
- The classroom is a place of learning. Concentrate hard on your own work and allow others to learn.
- Show respect to everyone.
- Treat others, their work and equipment with respect.
- Listen to the views or comments of others, even if different from your own.
- Eat only at break and lunchtimes, never in class.
- Use appropriate language at all times.
- Always acknowledge visitors to the class.
- Follow all instructions given.
- If in doubt, ask.
- Complete all work to the best of your ability.
- Present work neatly and accurately.
- All pieces of written work should have a date, whether the piece is class-work or prep and the title neatly underlined with a ruler.
- Expect to repeat or complete the work again if it is unsatisfactory.
- Punctuation, spelling and the good use of grammar is very important in all lessons.
- Keep books and your homework diary free from graffiti.
- Complete all prep and return it on time.
- Some parts of a lesson will include times of quiet, individual work. Some parts will require group work or class discussion (hands up).
- Pupils should only talk at appropriate times.
- Discussing non-subject related matters is a distraction and is not tolerated.

- Never shout out.
- Raise your hand before speaking.
- Stay seated at all times unless you are asked to move by the teacher.
- Do not rock on the chairs or sit on tables as this will cause damage.

Students should be made aware of the rule you set as a teacher from the offset. It may be wise to have them displayed in a prominent position in the classroom or you may also decide to provide each student with a copy of them to keep.

QUESTION 20

What are your classroom rules? How do you make students familiar with the rules?

Question 21 – *A student throws a pencil across the room. What do you do?*

At almost every interview you go to, you will be asked a classroom management question. As a teacher you will have a code of conduct to follow in relation to discipline. You should follow it at all times. In relation to this incident, it needs to be dealt with appropriately. There is a danger that the pencil, being a sharp object, could cause injury to another student. Therefore, you must act swiftly to prevent it from happening again.

Show that you will take responsibility for the management of the class until the situation is resolved.

Show that you have a stepped approach to dealing with the issue.

1. Speak to the student

2. Move them from their seat

3. Make them aware of the school policy

4. Issue a detention

In the end – this stepped approach leads to the Head of Department but you must show that you have followed the school policy and procedures to get there.

TOP TIP: Always make sure you are aware of school policy before the interview process.

QUESTION 21

A student throws a pencil across the room.
What do you do?

Question 22 – What would you do if a parent complained about an assignment?

This type of scenario may happen whilst you are employed as a teacher. Providing you are following the national curriculum, and the assignment is in the best interests of the student's development, you should try to persuade the parent that the assignment is beneficial. As the teacher you are in control of the development of the student; however, sometimes you will have to work hard in order to keep the parents on your side. You may decide to first of all listen to the parents' concerns. Once you have listened to their concerns you will then need to explain the reasons for the assignment. If the parent is still not happy then there will undoubtedly be a complaints procedure they can follow.

QUESTION 22

What would you do if a parent complained about an assignment?

Question 23 – If you are successful at interview, how long do you plan staying with our school?

When responding to this question you need to imply that you intend on staying with the school for a long time but be honest. Say that you have a plan to be a head of year or head of department. There is nothing wrong with showing ambition. It is pointless an educational organisation investing time, effort and resources into your training and development if you do not plan on staying with them. You have identified that this is the school you want to work for, and therefore you want to commit your future to them. It is also important for the students' development that they have consistency within class.

"I have looked into both this teaching role and the school and I have been impressed with the ambitions and plans and what has been achieved so far. With that in mind I plan to stay with you for a long time, if I am successful. Furthermore, I am serious about my application for this position and excited about the prospect of working with the passionate students who attend the school. I understand that you are going to be investing a lot of time, money and resources into my development and I would intend repaying that investment by being a loyal and competent employee."

Now use the template on the following page to create a response to this question that is based on your own opinions and beliefs.

QUESTION 23

If you are successful at interview, how long do you plan staying with our school?

Question 24 – *Why do you want to leave your current employment?*

This is a question that needs to be answered very carefully. It is not a good idea to state that you are leaving because of differences with a manager or member of the team. Or if you are already a teacher you do not want to raise any on-going disputes you may have with the school. It is far better to say that you are looking for new and fresh challenges and feel that you have achieved all that you can at your current employment.

Most people want a higher salary but it is also not a good idea to use this as a reason for your intention to move schools. By stating you would like a new challenge you will demonstrate drive and enthusiasm.

"Although I enjoy my current teaching job I am now ready for a new challenge. I have worked hard for my previous employer and they have been good to me in return. I have learnt an awful lot during my time with them but I am now in a position where I want to embark on new and fresh challenges. I will be leaving my current school with fond memories but I know the time is right for me to move on.

Having looked into your school and the role that I'm applying for I feel that I have so much to offer in terms of my experience, drive and enthusiasm and know that I would be a valuable asset to the teaching team."

Now use the template on the following page to create a response to this question that is based on your own views and opinions

QUESTION 24

Why do you want to leave your current employment?

Question 25 – *Why should we give you the job?*

You need to give the interview panel an answer that benefits them and not just yourself. Yes of course you are the best person for the job, but don't say it unless you can back it up with examples of why. Here are a few example of why you might be the best person for the job:

> Show willingness to be involved with extra-curricular activities, run sports teams or after hours clubs.

> BE CAREFUL – if you indicate you will do something like this, more often than not you will be asked to do it! Don't take too much on or put yourself down for something you have no real knowledge of!

> You have the ability to work in a pressurised environment and have a track record for achieving results. If you have been in a previous teaching role provide the panel with details of your successes.

> You are capable of achieving great things for their school and thrive under pressurised situations. For example, in your previous role you were given the task of implementing a new curriculum into your lesson plans at short notice and you achieved this with very positive results.

> You can make a positive impact on your students and have a track re-cord for delivering higher than average grades.

> You are a team player who has the experiences and skills to match the job description.

> You are loyal, hard-working and will act as a positive role model for their school.

> You are a creative teacher who is passionate about the role.

This type of question can make or break you and you should be prepared with a hard-hitting positive response. Be enthusiastic when responding and give brief examples of why you are the right person.

Now use the template below to create your own response.

QUESTION 25

Why should we give you the job?

Question 26 - One of your students is predicted a grade B but actually achieves a grade D – whose fault is it?

At the end of the day this is your responsibility however you must show that you have taken steps to ensure this student had every opportunity to achieve a grade B. There may be a number of factors and external influences beyond your control such as family issues or illness.

Again try to demonstrate a stepped approach to dealing with this issue;

- show that you have provided extra resources
- revision lessons
- spoken to parents
- spoken to the head of year and done everything possible to ensure that this student achieves a grade B.

"Ultimately the responsibility is with the teacher, however I feel that I have the necessary skills to ensure this wouldn't happen. It is extremely important that students, parents and the head of department are aware of any students that are not achieving their predicted grade. It would be my responsibility to identify the problem and put together a plan for success. This would include providing extra resources, ensuring revision lessons were provided, with the opportunity for mock exam preparation were grades can be monitored. I would also take steps to implement clear channels of communication between parents and members of staff informing them of progress.

As a passionate teacher with confidence in my ability I would always want to achieve and exceed my targets."

QUESTION 26

One of your students is predicted a grade B but actually achieves a grade D – whose fault is it?

Question 27 – *What qualities do you believe a good teacher should have?*

- A good teacher should know their subject well and make the lesson interesting through creative teaching.
- A good teacher should be a good listener and be passionate about the student's development.
- A good teacher should give boundaries and be firm yet fair.
- A good teacher should be able to install confidence in their class.
- A good teacher will be able to make their class feel at ease with difficult subjects and encourage them to ask questions when they are unsure.
- A good teacher will remain calm and never become aggressive.

Some other qualities of a good, competent teacher include:

- Having a positive attitude at all times
- Professionalism
- Organisational skills
- Punctual and flexible
- Confidence and excellent presentation skills
- Empathy and consideration
- Respectfulness
- Role model
- Non-discriminatory
- Creative
- Sense of humour

Now use the following template to create your own response to this question.

QUESTION 27

What qualities do you believe a good teacher should have?

Question 28 – Describe the most challenging student you've ever taught and how you dealt with them.

You may have to deal with challenging students at times during your career. Here are a few things to consider:

- Consider getting to the route of the problem. Why is the student behaving in a difficult manner?

- If they are challenging due to the fact they are struggling with the work, consider alternative ways to assist and support them.

- Consider using the school discipline route if alternative methods have failed.

- Consider involving the parents at the earliest opportunity.

QUESTION 28

Describe the most challenging student you've ever taught and how you dealt with them.

Question 29 – A parent writes a note and tells you that their daughter could not complete their homework assignment because she had a dance class the night before. What would you do?

This is a difficult situation; however, the school curriculum is more important that dance classes. Yes, these classes are important for the child's development but the school work must come first. You may consider speaking to the parent in order to establish how important the homework is in order to maintain the delivery of the school curriculum. What is important is that the homework is completed as soon as possible. It is also important to establish whether this incident is a one-off. If it is, then you may decide to not take any further action. However, if there is a danger that the incident could be repeated you need to take action to prevent it. Always involve the parents in incidents of this nature.

QUESTION 29

A parent writes a note and tells you that their daughter could not complete their homework assignment because she had a dance class the night before. What would you do?

Question 30 – Do you think it is appropriate for children in school to be using the Internet?

The internet has many positive aspects and also many negative aspects. Regardless of the negatives it is an essential part of everyday life. The use of the internet is only set to increase and therefore it is important that it is used during school as a tool for both teaching and for students to become proficient in its use. In order for a student to become competitive in the UK jobs market when they leave full-time education they need to be competent in the use of computers; therefore, they are essential.

Having said that, it is important their use is managed and supervised strictly in accordance with school policy and procedures.

QUESTION 30

Do you think it is appropriate for children in school to be using the Internet?

Question 31 – *What would you do to calm an angry parent?*

Firstly involve a senior member of staff or colleague and have them there to witness the conversation. In this type of situation it is best to employ effective communication skills. Consider taking the following action:

Listen

If you can think of nothing to say, stay quiet and listen to the outburst. Sometimes an angry person needs no more of an outlet than a one-man audience. Let them rant and rave and get their anger out, and hopefully the person can move on. It's hard to remember sometimes, but attentive silence is often the best way to cope with an angry person.

Stay Calm

Keep your anger under control. One of the two of you needs to keep a level head. If you get angry and frustrated, you won't be able to communicate properly with the person.

Remain Polite

Once again, if you are rude to an angry person, this is going to make matters worse. Remember you are a role model for the school.

Resolve and agree a solution

Look for a mutually beneficial resolution to the problem. Whatever you do, do not take it personally. You must try as hard as you can to remain calm throughout the situation.

QUESTION 31

What would you do to calm an angry parent?

Question 32 – Can you tell us about a situation when you have had to work under pressure?

Working under pressure is all part and parcel of being a teacher. The interviewer will therefore want to know that you have the ability to perform in such an environment. If you have experience of working under pressure then you are far more likely to succeed in a high-pressurised teaching role. When responding to a question of this nature, try to provide an actual example of where you have achieved a task whilst being under pressure.

"Within my previous school I was in charge of the mock interview process for our Year 10 students, which takes considerable organisation with administration staff, students, other teaching staff, caretakers, and of course employers.

I led a team to organise the whole day and we all had responsibilities but on the morning of the event, one of the administrators was ill, which meant we can no contact point for employers on the morning, or somebody to meet and greet and ensure they receive a positive experience of the school.

With only a couple of hours before the arrival of the employers we were stretched, so I spoke to the Deputy Head Teacher about bringing in a couple of Year 13 students to help support the event.

After this was agreed I spent time with the 2 students to explain what was required, the objectives and to give them a crash course in handling customers as well as encouragement as they were nervous.

During and after the event employers commented on the professionalism of the event, and also particularly the two students who helped support at short notice. The skills demonstrated, such as creating a positive first impression, communicating clearly and precisely won one of the students a part time job with an employer.

So from a extremely pressurised situation, by working as a team, placing trust in our students, we turned a negative position into a positive and further cemented relationships with the business community."

QUESTION 32

Can you tell us about a situation when you have had to work under pressure?

Question 33 – Can you provide us with an example of an educational project you have had to complete and the obstacles you had to overcome?

Having the ability to complete tasks and projects successfully demonstrates that you have the ability to persevere and complete tasks that will form part of your role as a teacher. Many people give up on things in life and fail to achieve their goals. The interviewer will want to be convinced that you are going to complete tasks successfully and, if you can provide evidence of where you have already done this, then this will go in your favour.

When responding to this type of question, try to think of a difficult, drawn out task that you achieved despite a number of obstacles that were in your way. You may choose to use examples from your work life or even from some recent academic work that you have carried out. Take a look at the following sample question before using the template provided to construct your own response based on your own experiences.

"Yes I can. I recently successfully completed a NEBOSH course (National Examination Board in Occupational Safety and Health) via distance learning. The course took two years to complete in total and I had to carry out all studying in my own time whilst holding down my current job.

The biggest obstacle I had to overcome was finding the time to complete the work to the high standard that I wanted to achieve. I decided to manage my time effectively and I allocated two hours every evening of the working week in which to complete the work required. I found the time management difficult but I stuck with it and I was determined to complete the course. In the end I achieved very good results and I very much enjoyed the experience and challenge. I have a determined nature and I have the ability to concentrate for long periods of time when required. I can be relied upon to finish projects to a high standard.

By investing time, financial resources and staying determined; achieving this qualification has benefited my previous school as I was able to carry out health and safety visits for work experience placements which saved the school considerable cost, as well as helping support the risk assessments for trips out for all year groups."

QUESTION 33

Can you provide us with an example of an educational project you have had to complete and the obstacles you had to overcome?

Now take a look at the following sample questions and responses before moving onto the next set of teaching interview questions and responses.

Question 34 – *How would you design the layout of your classroom?*

When answering a question like this you must be able to show flexibility – and that you can adapt the layout of your classroom for different types of lessons. Students will have to do exams/tests, group discussion, teamwork, and presentations. Give examples of different lay outs including; single desks, horse-shoe formations and tables nestled together for group activities. There are some important points to consider when setting up your classroom;

- Can all of the students see you?
- Can you move around the classroom easily to give guidance and monitor work?
- Can your students see your displays or board that you are using?
- Can your students interact with each other?

Furniture must be the appropriate size for the year group and students you are teaching, with each individual student having enough space to be able to work at.

Classroom displays need to be simple and clear and the space in your classroom should be uncluttered with well-placed furniture. You should also consider seating plans that will all assist you with your management of the classroom.

QUESTION 34

How would you design the layout of your classroom?

Question 35 – How would you plan a revision lesson?

Plan your revision lesson like you would plan any other lesson. Have clear, well defined and measurable objectives and make sure that your activities allow the students to achieve these objectives. It is also a good idea to include sample exam questions and advice on how to answer certain types of questions.

You need to assess the knowledge of students at the start of your lesson – through a quiz or group activity. Revision games also are a good way of motivating students and can allow you to recap prior knowledge and learning. However, you must make sure you consolidate learning and adapt your lesson to the student's knowledge. Include in your lesson revision tips and guides on how to revise.

QUESTION 35

How would you plan a revision lesson?

Question 36 – Describe the differences between a good teacher and a great teacher?

A good teacher is someone who follows the school curriculum and delivers the teaching/lesson plan to the best of their ability. A good teacher is someone who supports their students, provides quality teaching and carries out their work professionally, diligently and on time. A great teacher however is someone who excels at everything they do. They are extremely passionate and they have a natural ability for their craft. They involve students in the lesson plan and they come up with new and creative ways to teach. Their students are also passionate about their learning and they generally achieve above average grades in every subject.

QUESTION 36

Describe the differences between a good teacher and a great teacher?

Question 37 – How would you use data to monitor the progress of students you are teaching?

You must show that you are constantly monitoring and updating data to produce individualised learning plans.

You need to take action to make sure students are achieving targets and goals – use data to speak to parents, learning mentors, and heads of department to establish a plan of action for individual students.

Data can be used as a bench mark – share the information with students and make sure they are aware of what they can achieve.

TOP TIP: Teachers often only contact parents with negative or bad news. Teachers should contact parents with positive news and information to support and improve individual learning.

QUESTION 37

How would you use data to monitor the progress of students you are teaching?

Question 38 – *What are the mission and aims of this school?*

Many schools, colleges and universities set themselves missions, aims and objectives. These are sometimes in the form of a vision or charter. They usually relate to the high level of teaching and student care that they promise to deliver. When you apply for any teaching role you should not only prepare for each stage of the selection process but you should also learn as much as possible about the educational establishment you are applying to join. Learning this kind of information is important and it will demonstrate your seriousness about joining their particular school. Visit the website of the establishment you are applying for in order to view their mission, aims, objectives or customer charter.

The following is a sample fictitious customer charter

SAMPLE SCHOOL CHARTER

- Treat other people the way you wish to be treated.
- Take pride in yourself and your school with consideration for the School rules.
- Achieve your potential by working hard and making the most of what is available to you.
- Be individual and make your voice heard, but think of the consequences of what you say and do.
- Respect the property of the School and that of other people.
- Respect and preserve the environment.
- Support and include others within and outside the School community

---

Now use the template that follows to create a response to this question following your research into the educational establishment you are applying to join.

QUESTION 38

What are the mission and aims of this school?

Question 39 – Can you tell me about any achievements you have experienced during your life so far?

Those people who can demonstrate a history of achievement are far more likely to continue to succeed in their new working environment as a teacher. Having achieved something in your life demonstrates that you have the ability to see things through to the end, something that is crucial to your new career. It also shows that you are motivated and determined to succeed. Try to think of examples where you have succeeded or achieved something relevant in your life. Some good examples of achievements are as follows:

- Winning a trophy with a football or hockey team;
- GCSEs and other educational qualifications;
- Duke of Edinburgh's Award;
- Being given responsibility at work or at school;
- Raising money for charity.

"Yes I can. So far in my life I have achieved quite a few things that I am proud of. To begin with I achieved good grades whilst at school including a grade 'A' in English. I worked very hard to achieve my grades and I'm proud of them. At weekends I play rugby for a local team and I've achieved a number of things with them. Apart from winning the league last year we also held a charity match against the local Police rugby team. We managed to raise £500 for a local charity, which was a great achievement. More recently I managed to achieve a huge increase in my fitness levels. I have learnt that you have to work hard in life if you want to achieve things and I have a positive attitude to hard work. My own personal motto is 'work hard and you'll be rewarded'."

Now use the template on the following page to create a response based on your own skills and experiences.

QUESTION 39

Can you tell me about any achievements you have experienced during your life so far?

Question 40 – *How do you think your lesson went?*

As I stated earlier you will almost always be asked to teach a sample 30 – 40 minute lesson prior to your interview questions. After this you will almost certainly be asked how you thought your lesson went.

Think what you would improve – it is essential that you can show an interview panel that you can evaluate your own lesson and performance. However try to remain positive – say what you thought went well and be positive – show an interest in the students in the class. Remember to set clear objectives of what you want to achieve.

TOP TIP: remember individual student's names and highlight what certain students did well or could work on. John did this…Lucy needed extra support with…James did really well…

Think: *"What can the children now understand or do at the end that they couldn't do at the start?"* Remember to provide something for the students to do at the end of the lesson, extended time like which was discussed earlier. It may be an article or website!

QUESTION 40

How do you think your lesson went?

Question 41 – What would your approach be to teaching a mixed ability class?

Show joint planning with learning mentors, SEN coordinators and classroom assistants. Show and evidence differentiation in your lesson plans and demonstrate how you would put this into practise. Provide opportunities for the more advanced learners to consolidate their knowledge and share it with the group. Include all members of the group in a discussion on the theme early in your lesson and provide students with a variety of material to read on the theme.

You must also try to make sure the resources you use are at an appropriate level for each student. Set extension activities for students who may complete their tasks quickly and provide a more complex piece of work.

QUESTION 41

What would your approach be to teaching a mixed ability class?

Question 42 – *What didn't you like about your last job?*

If you are applying to move jobs into an external educational establishment then there will obviously be a reason why you want to move. We all have bad experiences in the working environment, and more often than not, the majority of people want to move simply because that either don't like their boss, or the people that they work with. Whatever you do, do not be disrespectful to any of your previous managers, teachers or work colleagues, no matter how much you disliked them! You should also avoid using salary as a motivating factor for moving jobs. I have heard some horror responses to this question during my time as an interviewer. Here's one of them:

"To be honest, I don't get on well with my boss. He treats me poorly and everyone in the office thinks he's a bully."

Whilst I didn't doubt the person's claims, I believe that any grievances should be kept to yourself. The key to answering this question successfully is to choose a genuine reason that shows you are motivated, and also that you want a new and fresh challenge.

"Basically I am ready for a new challenge. I have been in my previous role for seven years now and I feel the time has come for me to move on. I get on very well with my head teacher and the other members of staff in my team. Whilst I will miss them, I don't feel that I can develop any further in the same position. I am applying for this new job as I believe I can offer a great deal in terms of my skills and experiences. I am really looking forward to a new challenge and the benefits of working in a brand new environment."

Now use the template on the following page to create a response based on your reasons for moving jobs.

QUESTION 42

What didn't you like about your last job?

Question 43 – We presume that you have read the job description, so therefore which areas of the job appeal to you the least?

During an earlier section of this guide I explained how important it is to read and study the job description and person specification for the job. This question is one of the reasons why you must do just that! If you don't know what is contained within these important documents, then not only should you not be applying for the job, you'll also have no hope of answering the question.

Most interviewers will assess you against the job description for the teaching role you are applying for. The job description is basically a blueprint for the role that you are applying for and it determines the skills and attributes required to perform the job competently. Make sure you read the job description and also have examples ready of where you match each assessable area.

"Yes I have been studying the job description for some time now. To be honest, there aren't any elements that I wouldn't find appealing. To begin with, the requirement to deliver the curriculum to a very high standard is something that I would very much enjoy. I get a lot of satisfaction from teaching and supporting my students so this would not be a problem for me. The part in the description that requires you to maintain accurate reports and appraisals of all students is also not a problem. I am very organised and always complete tasks at the soonest opportunity. As mentioned already, there are no elements of the job description that I would dislike. I have carefully studied all elements and would relish the opportunity to work in this role."

Now use the template that follows to create a response based on your research of the job description for the role you are applying for.

QUESTION 43

We presume that you have read the job description, so therefore which areas of the job appeal to you the least?

Question 44 – We see there have been some gaps in your employment. Can you explain these?

If you have had any gaps in your employment then it is advisable that you have a valid reason for them. When responding to this type of question try to provide beneficial reasons for the gaps. Some good reasons for gaps in employment might be:

- Taking time off work to complete a study of development course
- Travelling to develop yourself or learn about a different language or culture
- Helping sick relatives or friends
- Carrying out voluntary work or community work

However, some not so good reasons for gaps in employment are:

- Getting over a previous stressful teaching job
- Going on holiday with your friends
- You fancied a break from teaching all together

The above will most probably put off a potential employer as there is a strong chance that you might want to leave them for a further gap in your employment.

"I took six months out from work to concentrate on finishing my Diploma educational course. I was eager to gain good grades so I decided to take a gap in my employment to fulfill this desire. It turned out to be a very good choice as I achieved excellent grades. I am passionate about personal development and as this is my chosen career path I continually want to improve and help support my students by introducing new methods and techniques in the classroom that will help them achieve excellent grades."

Now use the template that follows to create your own response to this question.

QUESTION 44

We see there have been some gaps in your employment.
Can you explain these?

Question 45 – How would you use a teaching assistant effectively?

To answer this question you must show that you can work together in planning, feedback and evaluation. Set clear goals for both of you and always remember to put your students first.

Show evidence of joint planning and share resources with the teaching assistant in your classroom. Try to establish a good relationship with the person you work with as this will only benefit the students.

You must not be afraid to seek specialised help and advice when you don't have the knowledge or expertise in a particular area. Often, teaching assistants have specialist training and will have experience in certain areas that you do not. Use this experience and work as a team.

QUESTION 45

How would you use a teaching assistant effectively?

Questions 46 – How would you demonstrate use of 'every child matters' in your lessons?

In order to answer this you need to identify opportunities to address ECM outcomes in both lesson plans and schemes of work. Include resources and activities that cover the main outcomes;

- to be healthy
- to stay safe
- to enjoy and achieve
- to make a positive contribution
- to achieve economic wellbeing

Show the interview panel how you have high professional values and have high expectations of your students, whilst building strong relationships and trust.

Create a positive classroom environment for your students, use praise and positive language and have routines to encourage learning.

Have clear and differentiated learning objectives and outcomes for your lessons and support the learning experience through contact with different teachers and adults outside of the classroom.

QUESTION 46

How would you demonstrate use of 'every child matters' in your lessons?

Question 47 – Do you have any final questions for the panel?

You've reached the end of the interview and the panel will now ask you a question similar to the above. How do you answer it without ruining your chances of success? I have seen people ruin their interview, simply by asking irrelevant and arrogant questions at the end. Be careful what you ask the panel and, if you do decide to ask questions, keep them to a minimum or two or three and ask questions that the panel can easily answer.

Take a look at the following sample responses:

"I appreciate that I am yet to find out whether or not I am successful, but is there anything I can read to prepare myself for the job, just in case I am successful?" This displays motivation and conscientiousness.

"I notice that you have introduced a new curriculum recently. Has this been a success?" This displays an enthusiastic interest in their school and the fact that you have carried out some research.

Now use the template on the following page to create your own response to this question.

QUESTION 47

Do you have any final questions for the panel?

OVERCOMING INTERVIEW NERVES

Many people who have an interview coming up will get nervous. Some people will unfortunately experience uncontrollable nerves. It is only natural to feel nervous before an interview, but there are a number of things that you can do to get over these nerves. To begin with, let's take a look at a few of the more common pre-interview anxieties:

- Feeling generally nervous and anxious
- Sweaty hands and palms
- Trembling voice
- Sore head
- Aching muscles
- Dry mouth
- Increased heart beat
- Shaky hands

It is only natural to expect one of the above symptoms of nervousness. The best advice is embrace it, it is a good sign! You just need to make sure you have done everything you can in your control to prepare for the day. Once you have done sufficient preparation for the interview, and you will know when that time has come, then it is pointless worrying anymore about it. Go into the interview feeling free, calm and relaxed, knowing you have given everything and enjoy the experience!

MOCK INTERVIEWS

Before I attend any interview I will always carry out a number of mock interviews. This basically involves getting friend or relative to sit down and ask me the anticipated interview questions under formal conditions. In fact, I even put on my suit during the mock interview to make it as realistic as possible. I have found over the years that this approach works extremely well in allowing me to improve my confidence, so make sure you try it!

VISUALISING THE INTERVIEW BEFORE YOU ATTEND IT

This is a great method that works for many people. Before you attend the interview, try and visualise the entire process. Sit down in your favourite armchair and close your eyes. Think about driving to the interview with plenty of time to spare. You arrive early at the interview venue and sit in the car park composing yourself and reading the job description. When you walk into the interview room you are standing tall, smiling and feeling relaxed and confident. You introduce yourself in a polite manner and shake the hands of each panel member. They immediately warm to you and your responses to the questions are both positive and inspiring. At the end of the interview you feel confident that you have done your absolute best and there is a strong possibility that you will be successful.

The above method is a fantastic way of focusing yourself prior to any interview. If you try to visualise the entire process being successful before the event starts, then this will put you in the correct frame of mind.

Good luck!

Antony Stagg & Diane Lloyd

CHAPTER 4
TEMPLATES AND EXAMPLE COVERING LETTER

Sample lesson plans and covering letters are outlined on the following pages.

SAMPLE LESSON PLAN

LEVEL:	Insert the level of the Diploma e.g. Foundation, Higher etc.	**DATE:**	Delivery date	**START TIME:**	Start of session
SUBJECT:	The specific subject should be entered here	**LOCATION:**	Where will the session take place	**DURATION (HOURS):**	Must be entered here
TUTOR:	Who is delivering the session?	**WMC WK No.:**	Insert the number	**SCHEME OF WORK REF:**	Session plan number as given in SOW
		QUAL. CODE:	From the SOW		

SESSION TOPIC: Title of the session

AIMS: An outline of the general aims of the session

LEARNING OUTCOMES: At the end of the session, learners will be able to: Consider differentiation - i.e.

1	Statement(s) of what will have been learned by the end of the session	4	At the end of the session, SOME learners will be able to:
2		5	etc - as appropriate
3		6	e.g. - At the end of the session, a few learners will...

HIGHLIGHT HOW DIFFERENTIATION WILL BE ACHIEVED: Tick each box as appropriate

RESOURCES
e.g. graduated task sheets O materials adaptation O other please specify _____

TASK SETTING
e.g. graded exercises O choice of tasks O tasks with a variety of outputs O extension tasks O other please specify _____

SUPPORT
e.g. learning support O hints & tips O "engineered" groups" O individual target setting O 1:1 support O other please specify _____

ASSESSMENT
e.g. targeted questioning O peer assessment O self assessment O other please specify _____

FEEDBACK
e.g. written O oral O group O peer O individual O other please specify _____

TIME	LEARNING ACTIVITY	LEARNING OUTCOME	RESOURCES	ASSESSMENT	FUNCTIONAL SKILLS/PLTS REF.
Indicate actual times when learning activities will take place (Inspection requirement). If the No of minutes is preferred as well, ensure Curriculum Area consistency.	Teaching & learning strategies should include a variety of methods Differentiation should be evident in order to meet individual learner needs and challenge all learners in the group. Methods of differentiation include: task, support, feedback, assessment, etc Refer to Every Child Matters where appropriate If the activity involves the use of IT (interactive whiteboard, digital projector) please make a specific reference of any intended use Where appropriate, indicate anything relating to assignment / assessment	Relate each activity to the table above by number (1,2,3 etc.)	Identify eg flip charts / pens, handouts, worksheets, practical resources	eg – written work, self-assessment, oral questioning, observation	Use Functional Skills and PLTS reference codes Do not include too many – References included on Lesson Plan should show how they are being assessed
ADDITIONAL SUPPORT:	If this takes place – Note how the LST / LSA will be involved. How learning materials are to be adapted. LST / LSA should receive their own copy of the Lesson Plan				
INDEPENDENT LEARNING:	Homework * Research required etc.				
EXTENSION ACTIVITIES:	Identify the activities that will stretch the more able learners				

SAMPLE LESSON PLAN CONTINUED

POST-SESSION EVALUATION: Include teaching, learning and attainment & suggested improvements

Complete as soon as possible after the session and address the actions for the next relevant session

(To be completed at the end of the class)

Were learning outcomes achieved? If not how is this to be addressed?

How successful was the teaching and learning approach?

Any problem areas?

Any changes needed for future sessions?

Any learner feedback

Any LSA feedback?

LESSON PLAN CHECKLIST

Use the chart categories below to indicate each:

Activity / Resource / Method that will check learning in this session; and to show the: Structure of the Session / Teaching & Learning

WORK RELATED ACTIVITIES	✓	RESOURCES	✓	METHODS TO CHECK	✓
Demonstration		Board		Written Work	
Discussion		Flip Chart/Pens		Tutor Observation	
Research		Worksheets or handouts		Self Assessment	
Practical/Work Shop		Interactive white board		Peer Assessment	
Guest Speaker		DVD/CD ROM Player		Written Assessment	
Site Visit		Computers/IT Room		Oral Questioning	
Group Work		PowerPoint		Checklist	
Role Play		Realistic Working Environment		Assignment	
Simulation		Employers Premises		Other:	
Other:		Other:			

STRUCTURE OF SESSION	✓	TEACHING/LEARNING	✓
Welcome and introduction		Learning objectives & appropriate tasks identified	
Review of previous work/ matters outstanding		Learning objectives & outcomes shared	
Objectives/structure of the session		Opportunities for whole, group or paired discussion related to learning	
Update on relevant developments		Pupils encouraged to listen & learn from each other	
		Progress, in relation to objectives , is reviewed with the class	

SAMPLE COVERING LETTER

Two sides of A4, no spelling errors or punctuation, get someone to proof read, tailor to the school you are applying, look at their website and Ofsted report. Don't fill in the section on the application form just attach your covering letter.

Although our example goes over 2 pages, this is give you more ideas to think about when compiling your letter. (MAKE SURE IT IS TWO.)

Mr /Ms
Headteacher
Example High School
Example Road
Town
Postcode

Dear Mr/Ms

Further to your recent advertisement in the TES?, I am writing to apply for the position of *subject* Teacher. Currently I am studying for a PGCE in *subject* at _____ University.

My PGCE course has given me the knowledge to deliver *what* in terms of *subject knowledge, ie national curriculum, A level teaching, GCSE. What are the main learning areas on the course, ie SEN, Classroom Management, lesson planning, assessment. The big issues currently i.e. ECM, :AFL, APP, target set-ting, project/extended project, 14-19. etc. State that the PGCE you have un-dertaken has given you credits towards a masters and any major pieces of work that you think are worth mentioning including if relevant your undergraduate dissertation. Are you a member of any subject associations ie EBEA (econom-ics and business education association)*

My teaching placements have been as follows:

Placement name, age group ie an 11-16 school, a college. On this placement I was involved in teaching ? to which age group, which qualification. Did you do anything else in this placement i.e. parents evening, after school activities, staff meeting, etc. You need to demonstrate you were involved in the life of the school and you used your time there to actively become part of the school/college. What did you learn on this placement about assessment, target setting, classroom management, subject etc.

My second teaching placement was *placement name, type of school/college,*

Age group. During this placement I taught at key stages ? and ?. You need to say whether you team taught or did some individual. What year groups, sets and what courses ie BTEC, GCSE diploma, A Level Did you do form teacher, who to? What about PSHE, year group and topic.

My final placement was/is at *need to say where and update when you have done it with details of what taught there. Again anything you did other than subject teaching.*

If you think your previous experience has been of benefit to your teaching and learning say how. *E.g. My industry experience has been valuable in enabling me to plan curriculum where learners are given opportunities to apply their knowledge Have you used any of your particular expertise gained in industry during your teaching practice, if so say how? Did you do any teaching experience before coming on the PGCE course, if so say what it was and how long for.*

During my PGCE I opted to take an additional course of study to prepare for diploma teaching. This is very much based on applied learning pedagogy as well as the design and delivery of the diploma itself. I have experience of the generic aspects of the diploma and feel confident in embedding functional skills and personal, learning and thinking skills within lessons.

What sort of person are you and what else can you offer the school.
E.g. I am a highly self-motivated, enthusiastic individual with the ability to adapt to any role within the school environment. I enjoy working as a team and I have found that this is a key part of successful teaching, being prepared to share ideas and work together for the benefit of the learners. What else can you offer a school ie after school science club, revision classes after school for students, sport, industry links which they could use, trips for students to industry. Look on the website for examples of the what the school does that you could become involved in. Do you have any relevant competencies that might be relevant eg first aid, youth work, summer camps.

What is you vision for education in particular reference to your subject are. Why do you want to teach? What do young people gain from your subject area?

End on a positive note. You look forward to showing your expertise at interview. You will work hard to ensure that you complete your NQT year and work towards completing your masters. Show that you are interested in professional development

Yours sincerely

Signature

GOOD EXAMPLE COVERING LETTER

Dear Mr _____

Further to your recent advertisement in the TES, I am writing to apply for the Teacher of ICT post in your school. I have very recently completed my PGCE in Applied ICT (14-19) at _____ University.

I have chosen a career in teaching so I can pass on the knowledge I have gained from my studies during my own education and my experiences in industry and I realise the impact that various teachers have made upon my life. I am very keen to give pupils an understanding of how ICT can enhance their learning and how it links with everyday functionality, thus it has been my abiding ambition to enter the teaching profession and inspire others, as I have been inspired. I am a self-motivated, hard working and enthusiastic individual with the ability to adapt to any role within a learning environment. I enjoy working in a team and I have found that this is a key part of successful teaching, being prepared to share ideas and work together for the benefit of the learners. I can offer the school additional support including extracurricular and cross-curricular activities and revision sessions out of timetable and I am very keen to develop industry links for educational use.

I came to the end of my final year at _____ University in July 2007 completing a BSc Honours Degree in Information Systems. I have successfully gained a 2:1 classification within my degree subject.

My PGCE course has given me the skills to deliver a wide variety of subject knowledge within the 11-19 national curriculum including ICT for Life, BTEC National Diploma's, Edexcel and OCR Functional Skills, GCSE and A Level. During my PGCE I followed an applied route of learning which has given me insights into the practical learning environment. There is a variety of learning areas within my PGCE that I have developed during my teaching placements; these include lesson planning, classroom management, behaviour management and I am experienced in the assessment of coursework and assessing pupil's progress. I have worked closely with a number of pupils with learning difficulties including ADHD, Dyslexia, deafness and Aspergers syndrome and with pupils, whose English is a second language.

During my PGCE I undertook two teaching placements. My first placement was at _____ College. In this placement, I was involved in teaching on the BTEC Level 2 Diploma in Information Technology and

Edexcel Functional Skills at Level 2. During this teaching placement, I feel that I developed my communication skills with SEN and EAL students.

My final teaching placement was at _____ High School. On this placement, I have been involved in teaching on the BTEC National and First Diplomas in Information Technology at level two and three, across key stage four and five and ICT for life in key stage 3. I have also taken on the role of a form tutor, which allows me to work with a year 7 form group.

I have also been to a feeder primary school to assist in the deliverance of eSafety and cyber bullying and how this has an effect within society. I attended a 'Computing for Schools' sixth form conference called 'Inventing the Future' with a selection of pupils from the school, which I co-coordinated. This was an interesting trip to organise, as I was able to work with pupils in an out-of-school context, encourage pupils to take up a career in computing and be part of something that I enjoy. Along with this, I have also gained and delivered BBC News School Report training, an annual project that thousands of pupils in UK schools learn and become broadcasters for the day. I would be very interested in developing these links within you school. I have begun to develop ideas linked to the development of the ICT Club and have been looking into the different subjects within ICT that have been developed in the past ready for September. Again, I have been involved in the whole school teaching life and I find this both invigorating and reflective in terms of professional development.

To conclude, I am adaptable to new ideas, but I will also bring my own ideas with me and that capacity for flexibility and professional innovation will, I am certain, be a purposeful and constructive asset to your school.

Thank you for your time in this matter and I look forward to hearing from you in the near future.

Yours sincerely

Signature

**Visit www.how2become.co.uk to find more titles and
courses that will help you to pass any job interview or
selection process:**

- Online psychometric testing
- Job interview DVDs and books
- 1-day intensive career training courses
- Psychometric testing books and CDs.

WWW.HOW2BECOME.CO.UK

THE **TESTING** SERIES